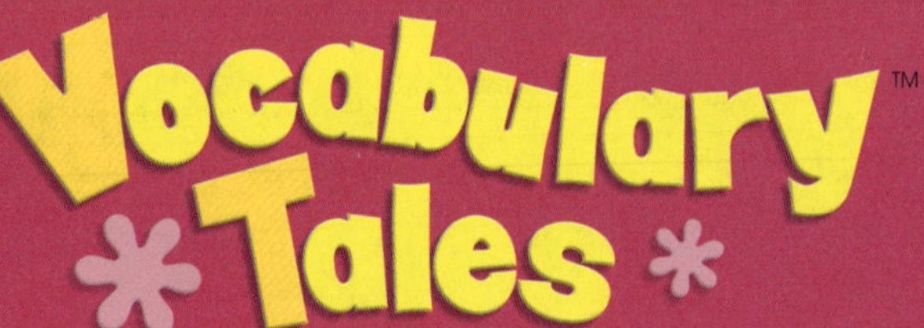

Seymour the Scaredy-Shark

by Pamela Chanko
illustrated by Jackie Stafford-Snider

SCHOLASTIC INC.

New York • Toronto • London • Auckland • Sydney
Mexico City • New Delhi • Hong Kong • Buenos Aires

Designed by Maria Lilja
ISBN-13: 978-0-545-08853-4 • ISBN-10: 0-545-08853-4

First printing, November 2008
12 11 10 9 8 7 6 5 4 3 2 1   8 9 10 11 12 13/0

Building Vocabulary With This Book

This book contains eight key words that are important for all children to know. Read the story straight through for enjoyment. Then read it again, pausing to define and discuss each key word. Follow-up the tale with the fun activities on pages 14–16. When you're done, celebrate—kids will have added eight great words to their vocabularies!

Seymour was a scaredy-shark.
The ocean scared him. It was dark!

Seymour found the big blue **sea**
a deep and spooky place to be.

KEY WORD: **seaweed**

Simple Definition: a plant that grows in the sea

Sample Sentence: You can sometimes see *seaweed* floating in the ocean.

Seaweed made him quite upset.
It felt so slimy—and so wet!

Seashells made him run and hide.
You never knew who lived inside!

And when an octopus came near,
he hid behind his **fins** in fear.

When dolphins came to splash and play,
Seymour simply swam away.

KEY WORD: scales

Simple Definition: the small pieces of hard skin that cover the body of a fish, snake, or other reptile

Sample Sentence: Some fish have *scales* that are many different colors.

Seymour was afraid of whales,
and eels and snails and fish with **scales**.

So everywhere that he would swim,
the animals made fun of him.

But Sam the shrimp, his only friend,
would stick by Seymour to the end.

So Seymour knew he must be brave
when Sam got trapped inside a **wave**!

He held his breath and took a **dive**.
And Seymour got Sam out alive!

And then it spread from sea to **shore**,
that Seymour was afraid no more!

Meaning Match

Listen to the definition. Then go to the WORD CHEST and find a vocabulary word that matches it.

1. shells of sea animals

2. a raised part of the water that moves and rolls

3. the land along the edge of an ocean, river, or lake

4. to go headfirst into the water

5. the ocean

6. a plant that grows in the sea

7. the small pieces of hard skin that cover the body of a fish, snake, or other reptile

8. parts on the body of a fish that flap and are used for moving through the water

Answers: 1. seashells 2. wave 3. shore 4. dive 5. sea 6. seaweed 7. scales 8. fins

Vocabulary Fill-ins

Listen to the sentence. Then go to the WORD BOX and find the best word to fill in the blank.

WORD BOX

seashells	dive	scales	wave
seaweed	fins	sea	shore

1. The water was so clear that I could see green __________ growing up from the bottom.

2. I want to learn how to surf, so I can ride on a __________.

3. Snakes and fish both have __________ on their bodies.

4. If you want to collect __________, make sure there are no animals still living inside them!

5. A fish swims by flapping its __________.

6. My swimming teacher showed me how to __________ off the edge of the pool.

7. Have you ever swum in the salty __________?

8. Everyone stood on the __________ to watch the boat race.

Answers: 1. seaweed 2. wave 3. scales 4. seashells 5. fins 6. dive 7. sea 8. shore

Vocabulary Questions

Listen to each question. Think about it. Then answer.

1. Pretend you are a shark using your **fins** to swim through the water. Where will you go? What will you see?

2. Would you rather have skin or **scales** like a fish? Tell why.

3. Can you think of five great words to describe **seashells**?

4. Have you ever felt **seaweed**? What did it feel like? If not, what do you think it would feel like?

5. What animals live in the **sea**? Make a list.

6. Would you rather **dive** into a pool or jump in feetfirst? How come?

7. Imagine you are standing in the ocean and a giant **wave** washes over you. How do you feel (besides wet!)?

8. What are some things you might find on the **shore** of an ocean? How about a lake or river?

Extra: Can you think of some more ocean words? Make a list.